FUN PRODUCT IDEAS

Preface

This collection of fun and innovative product concepts is the culmination of five years of creativity, passion, and a relentless pursuit of fun and innovative product ideas. As you embark on this journey with me, allow me to share the story behind this endeavor and the inspirations that fueled my imagination. My motivation for writing this book arose from the desire to bring together all of my ideas under one roof. Over the past five years, I have been captivated by the world of product design, constantly envisioning unique concepts that may never see the light of day in terms of production or sales. However, this book is a testament to the power of creativity, the joy of ideation, and the ability to infuse imagination into everyday objects. Curiously, my passion for design and innovation developed quite unexpectedly. I never considered myself a naturally creative person, having never engaged in activities typically associated with art or design. It all began during a university course on advertising when an assignment sparked something within me. The task was to create a fun promotion for a product, and that's when the idea for a soap bottle design that turns into soap bubbles was born.

Despite veering from the professor's intended direction, the response was overwhelmingly positive, and a spark ignited. From that moment on, I continued down the path of product design, generating nearly 50 unique ideas over the next five years purely for the joy of it. What motivated me to explore and conceive these unconventional product ideas was the belief that products can transcend mere functionality. They can be cool, enjoyable, and still address the problem they aim to solve. Creativity and playfulness set products apart from their competitors. Take Dyson vacuum cleaners, for instance. Who would have thought that a vacuum cleaner could be someone's most beloved possession? Yet, Dyson achieved this by infusing fun and innovation into their designs, resulting in products that are highly functional and bring joy to their users.

Through this book, my hope is that readers will discover the sheer pleasure of product design. It's an invitation to explore the realm of creativity, where innovative concepts can spark the imagination and redefine conventional expectations. Each page aims to inspire, reminding us that there is room to break free from the monotony of identical designs. I find great satisfaction in offering a fresh perspective, whether through the packaging, the product itself, or by adding a whimsical twist. I have a deep aversion to anything mundane or uninspired, and this book is a celebration of the extraordinary.

While I acknowledge that I am not a professional product designer, this book is intended for anyone seeking inspiration. It is an tribute to my years of work, a personal endeavor to capture these ideas, and a testament to the power of imagination. Perhaps one day, my daughter will come across this book, and it will make her proud of her father's creative journey, and who knows, maybe it will inspire her too. Lastly, I want to acknowledge that my design skills are limited. The concepts presented in this book were brought to life by talented outsourced designers, whom I entrusted with illustrating my ideas. Their contributions have helped transform my visions into tangible designs that now grace the pages before you. So, dear reader, immerse yourself in the vibrant world of product design concepts. Let these ideas spark your own imagination, and may this book serve as a reminder that creativity knows no bounds.

Can Lid Opener

Departing from the standardized opener shape seen across canned food and beverages, this idea brings a delightful twist to the packaging. Imagine opening your tuna can with a fish-shaped handle, or your dog food can with a paw-shaped opener, or even a pineapple-shaped opener for your canned pineapple. By infusing these distinct lid openers based on the ingredients inside, this concept offers a fun and memorable experience for consumers. this innovative design not only adds a playful element to an item that has remained unchanged for decades but also serves as a rebranding opportunity. In a marketplace where similarities abound, these whimsical lid openers allow your products to stand out from the crowd.

Dual-Sided Ketchup

Introducing a playful and innovative concept for ketchup bottles: a dual-sided design that revolutionizes the way you enjoy your favorite condiment. Say goodbye to the frustration of banging on the bottom of the bottle or struggling to get that last drop of ketchup out. With this unique bottle, you can squeeze from any side you desire, ensuring easy access to your beloved ketchup at all times.

No more wasted ketchup! The dual-opening design allows for effortless dispensing, regardless of the bottle's orientation. Whether it's stored upright, sideways, or even upside down in the fridge, you'll always have a smooth flow of ketchup ready to enhance your meals. But why stop at ketchup?

Imagine the possibilities of a dual-sided bottle that combines both ketchup and mustard compartments. With this single bottle, you can effortlessly switch between condiments, adding a burst of flavor to your hot dogs, burgers, and more. No need for multiple containers cluttering your table or fridge. This concept not only offers practicality and convenience but also brings an element of fun and creativity to your dining experience. Just imagine the joy of flipping the bottle and squeezing out the perfect blend of ketchup and mustard, adding an exciting twist to your favorite dishes.

HEINZ
ESTᴰ 1869 ESTᴰ
TOMATO
KETCHUP
57 VARIETIES
GROWN NOT MADE

The Forget-Proof Key

Introducing "The Forget-Proof Key" – a smart and simple solution to the age-old problem of wondering if you locked your house door. We've all been there, rushing out of the house and then questioning ourselves, "Did I lock the door?" It's a moment of uncertainty that can nag at you all day. But worry no more! With this innovative key, you'll never have to wonder again. It features a special mechanism that visually indicates the last action performed on your door lock. When you turn the key to the right and lock the door, a red lock symbol appears on top of the key, providing a clear and reassuring sign that your door is securely locked. Alternatively, when you turn the key to the left and unlock the door, a green unlock symbol displays on the key, confirming that your door is open. The intuitive visual cues take the guesswork out of your home security, making sure you're always in the know. Say goodbye to the anxiety of second-guessing and the hassle of returning home just to check if your door is locked. While there are more technologically advanced options available, such as apps or keycards, they often come with higher costs and may require additional changes to your existing door lock system. This key, on the other hand, offers an affordable and efficient solution without the need for expensive upgrades.

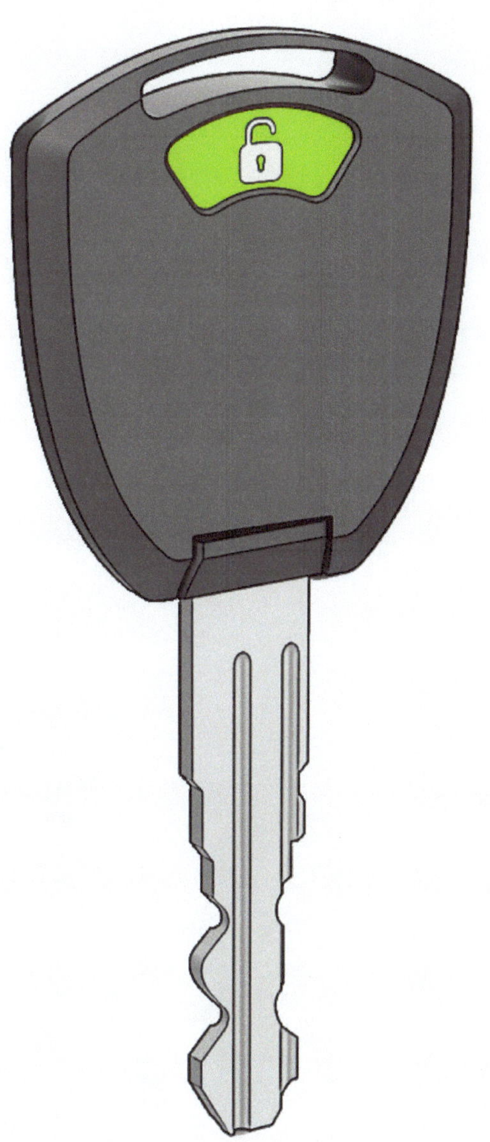
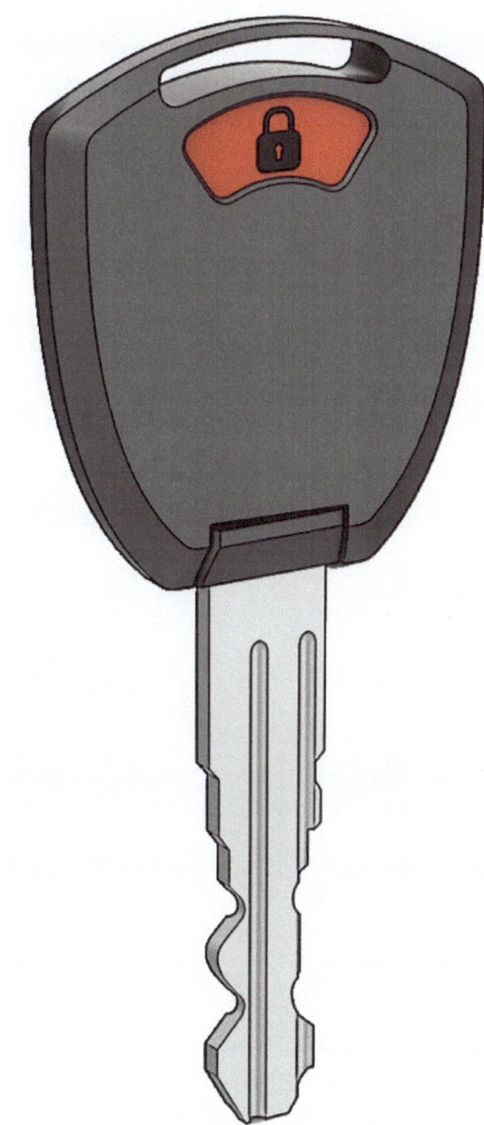

Pot Heat Indicator

Introducing a smart and thoughtful innovation for kitchen safety – the heat-sensitive cooking pot. This creative concept draws inspiration from the popular heat-sensitive mugs, aiming to make your kitchen a safer place for the whole family, especially for small kids. Consider a cooking pot that effortlessly conveys its hot surface through a unique visual cue. This thoughtful concept is purposefully designed to prevent kitchen mishaps and grant you reassurance during your cooking adventures.

At the heart of this concept lies a clever visual indicator. As you heat the cooking pot, a unique "red crossed circle with a hand inside" symbol discreetly appears on the surface, clearly signaling that the pot is hot. This intuitive and eye-catching design instantly warns everyone in the kitchen about the potential danger, allowing them to avoid accidental burns.

With the heat-sensitive cooking pot, you can enjoy the pleasure of preparing delicious meals while prioritizing the safety of your loved ones. No more second-guessing whether the pot is too hot to touch or accidentally exposing yourself or your children to burns. This innovative kitchen tool seamlessly integrates safety into your cooking routine, making it effortless to keep a watchful eye on the pot's temperature.

Head to your kitchen right now and envision creative solutions for common kitchen challenges. With a touch of creativity, elevate your kitchen experiences, making cooking safer, more enjoyable, and remarkably inventive. Remember, it all starts with a simple idea – a visual cue that speaks volumes. The heat-sensitive cooking pot is proof that creativity knows no bounds.

Umbrella Stand

This idea provides a practical and aesthetically pleasing solution. When hanging your umbrella on this stand, the water droplets naturally fall onto the plant pot beneath, simultaneously nurturing your plants and drying your umbrella.

This unique design offers a convenient and visually appealing way to handle wet umbrellas while adding a charming touch to your home decor.

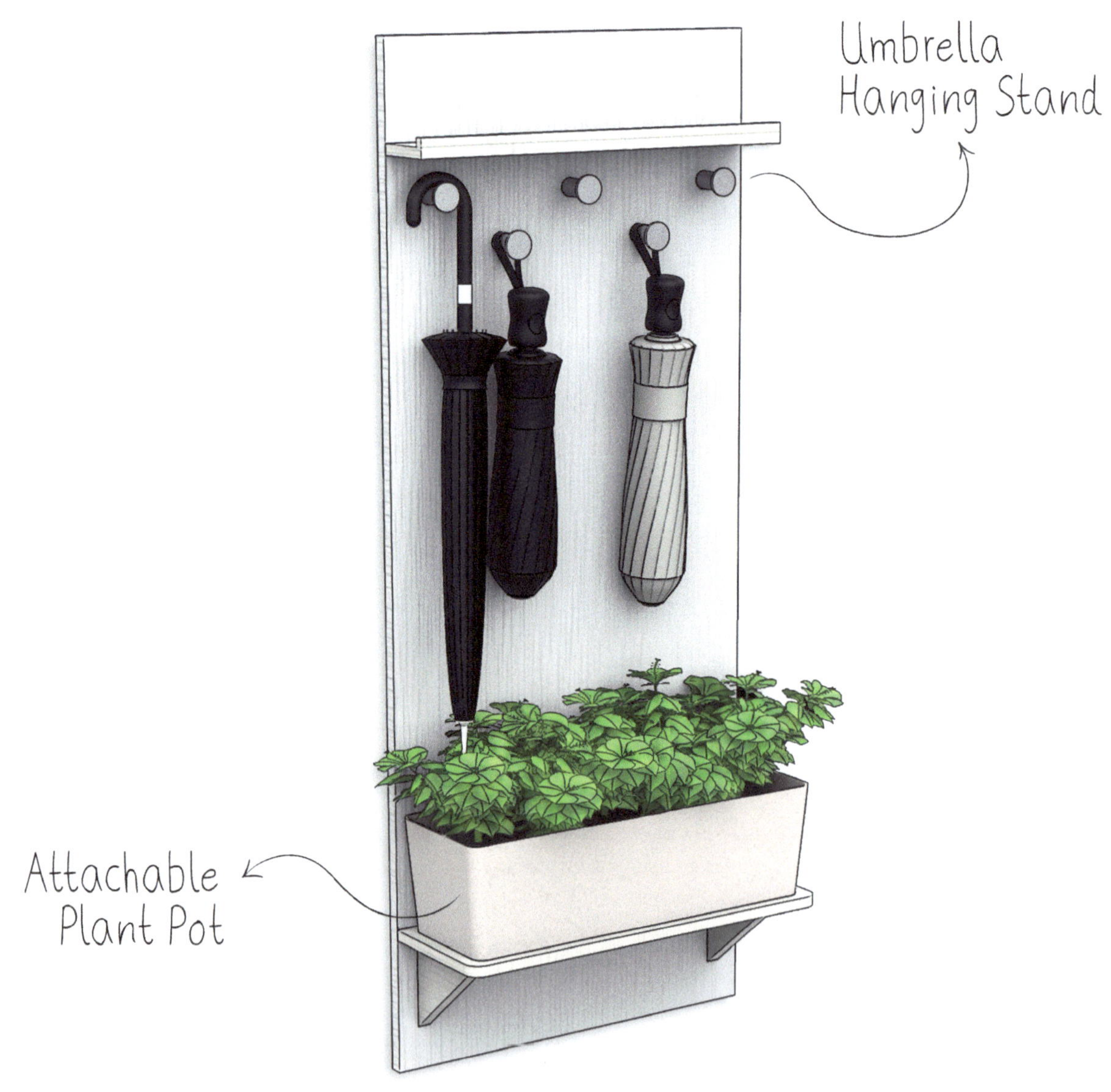

Laundry Shelf

The Universal Base transforms the laundry room into a space of efficiency and inspiration. With its thoughtfully crafted design, this innovative concept provides a practical solution for separating your washing machine and dryer. Placing your laundry basket on the removable wooden shelf streamlines the process of transferring clothes from the dryer, eliminating unnecessary back-and-forth movements. It's a remarkable lesson in creativity and timing - as I developed this idea and finalized the design, I discovered that a similar product already existed online. It served as a valuable reminder that success often lies not in being the first to conceive an idea, but in being the first to bring it to market. The Universal Base exemplifies the power of transforming everyday tasks into moments of ingenuity, making your laundry routine efficient, convenient, and aesthetically pleasing.

Custom Bin Pocket

Introducing a fun and space-saving solution that combines a trash bin with a built-in pocket to store plastic bags effortlessly. No more buying separate dispensers or dealing with cluttered plastic bags! With this creative concept, you can easily keep your plastic bags within reach while also keeping your space organized and efficient.

The "Custom Bin Pocket" features a convenient front pocket on the trash bin, specially designed to neatly hold plastic bags. Now you can reuse and store your bags in one place without the need for additional storage solutions. It's a smart and practical way to declutter your home while promoting eco-friendly practices.

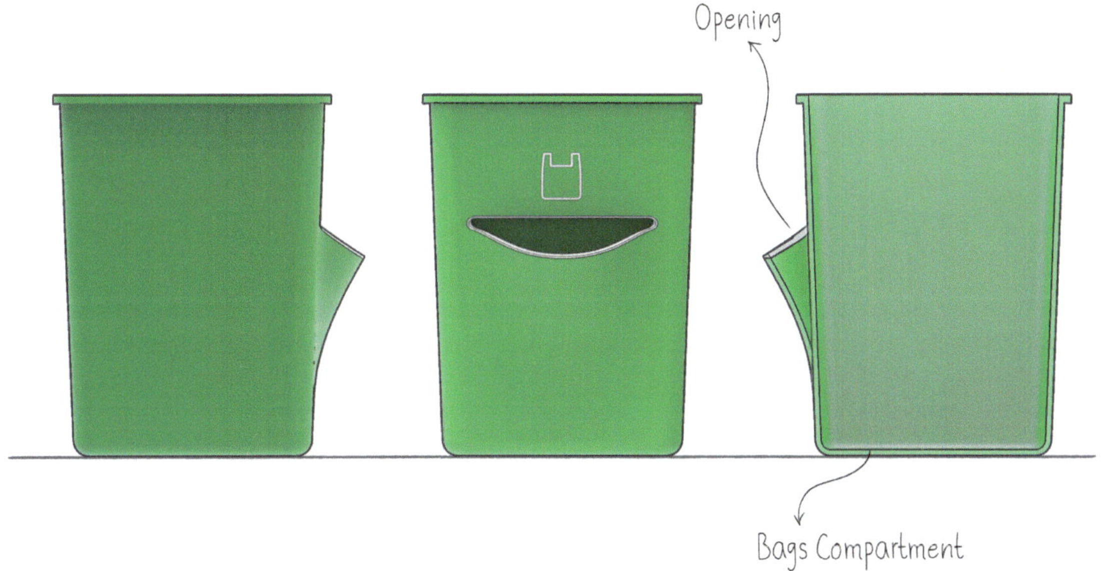
Opening
Bags Compartment

Trash Bin
Built In Pocket
for Bags

Anti-Spill Toilet Brush

The traditional design, with its water-storing head, often results in messy and unhygienic experiences, leaving bathroom floors wet and unsanitary. This innovative idea aims to reinvent the toilet brush, providing a solution that is both practical and efficient. The core of this concept lies in a detachable toilet brush head, strategically located inside the toilet, just beneath the water flow area. With every flush, the brush head gets rinsed and cleaned, eliminating the need for stagnant water storage.

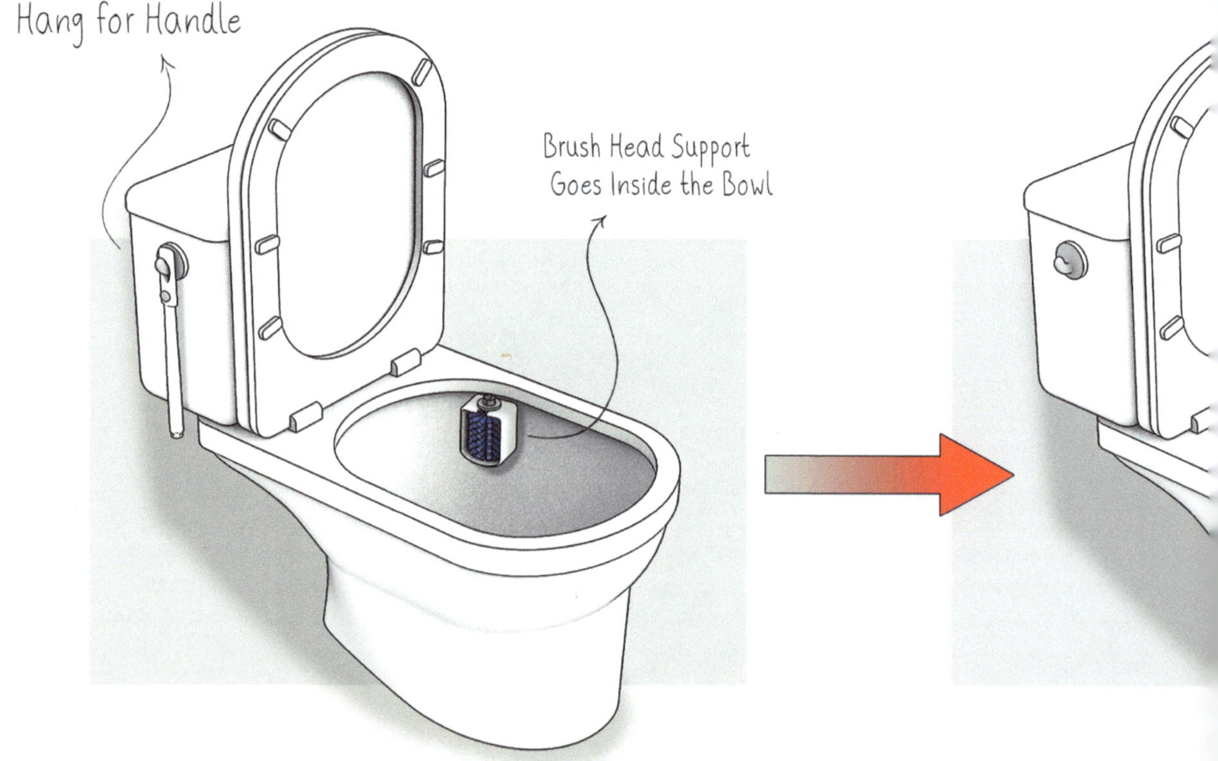

Say goodbye to the hassle of back-and-forth transfers that spread toilet water around the bathroom. The handle features a smart and functional design. When not in use, the handle hangs neatly by the side of the toilet, making it easily accessible.

When it's time to clean, the handle detaches and securely attaches to the brush head inside the toilet. This user-friendly approach streamlines the cleaning process, making it seamless and hygienic.

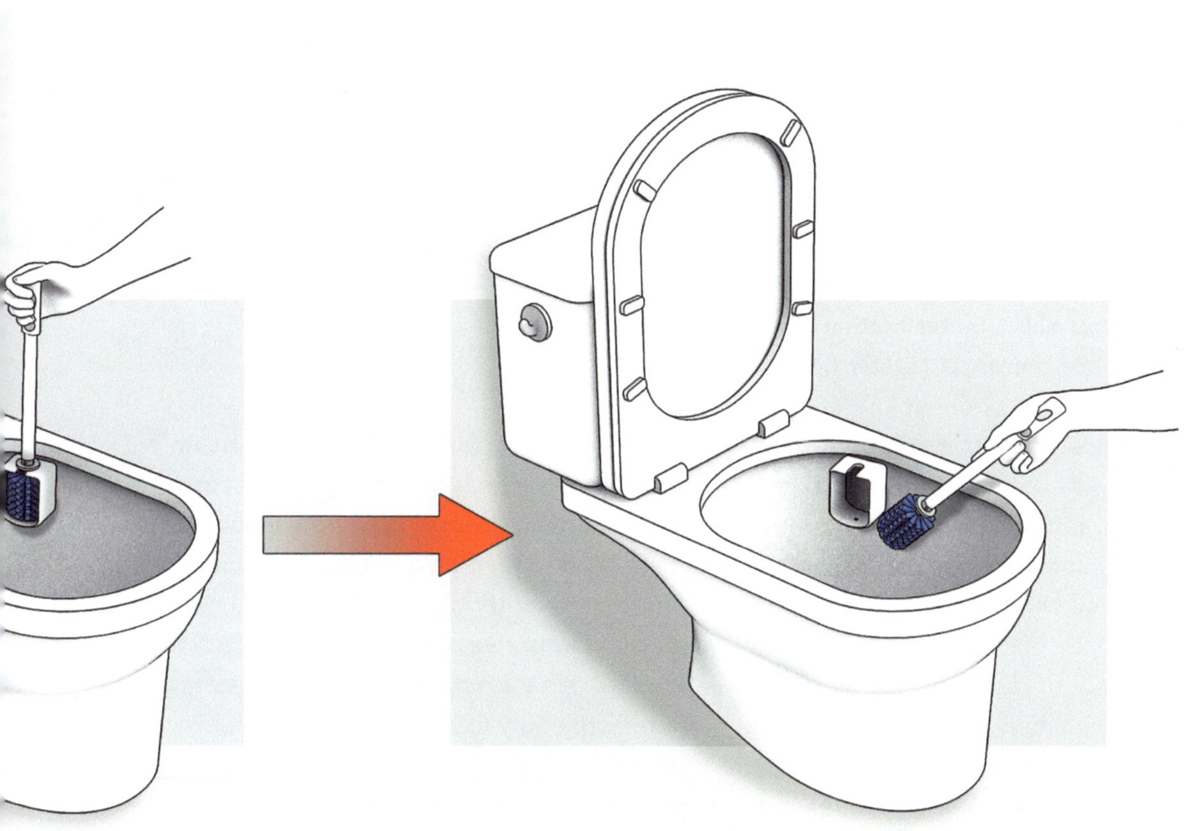

Recycled Water Gun

As part of my creative process, I enjoy challenging myself to find innovative solutions to various tasks. During one of these creative endeavors, I decided to explore the realm of recycling. With the abundance of empty bottles in my household, I sought to find a unique and creative purpose for them. The phrase 'extending a product life cycle' which refers to the practice of prolonging the usefulness and value of a product beyond its original intended purpose or lifespan resonated with me, inspiring the idea of repurposing these bottles into something engaging and fun. The concept that emerged from this exploration was a water gun design that could transform any empty bottle into a fully functional water-gun. Living in a hot climate, I observed children in my neighborhood playing with water guns, and it struck me as a perfect opportunity to merge recycling and playfulness. By creating a water gun with a unique nozzle attachment, which could be easily screwed onto the standard opening of any bottle, I envisioned a versatile and eco-friendly toy. The design accommodates both small and large bottle sizes, catering to the needs of children of different ages. The smaller 0.5-liter bottles are ideal for younger kids, while the larger 1.5-liter bottles provide a more substantial option for older children. This inclusivity ensures that kids of all ages can enjoy the fun and excitement of water play while actively participating in the recycling process. Not only does this concept promote recycling and extend the life cycle of plastic bottles, but it also presents an opportunity to educate children about the importance of responsible consumption through play and enjoyment. By combining recycling and fun, we can engage young minds and foster a deeper understanding of environmental sustainability. The water gun design allows for creativity and customization, as children can

decorate their repurposed bottles with vibrant colors and personal designs. This aspect adds an element of self-expression and encourages kids to take pride in their unique water gun creations.Ultimately, the water gun concept serves as a reminder that innovative and eco-friendly solutions can be found in everyday items. It offers a playful and interactive way to teach children about recycling, while simultaneously providing them with hours of enjoyment under the sun. Let's empower the next generation to make a positive impact on our environment, one water gun adventure at a time."

Instant Cat Feeder

Presenting the "Instant Cat Feeder" – a creative solution to provide a hygienic and convenient feeding spot for stray cats. With an estimated one million stray cats in our country and numerous cat lovers like myself caring for them, this concept aims to transform regular trash cans into practical feeding stations. the design features a small metal tray with hooks that effortlessly attach to the holes commonly found in trash cans. In just moments, the "Instant Cat Feeder" securely rests on the trash can, instantly creating a designated and elevated feeding spot for our furry friends. No more scattering food on the ground or dealing with complaints from others.

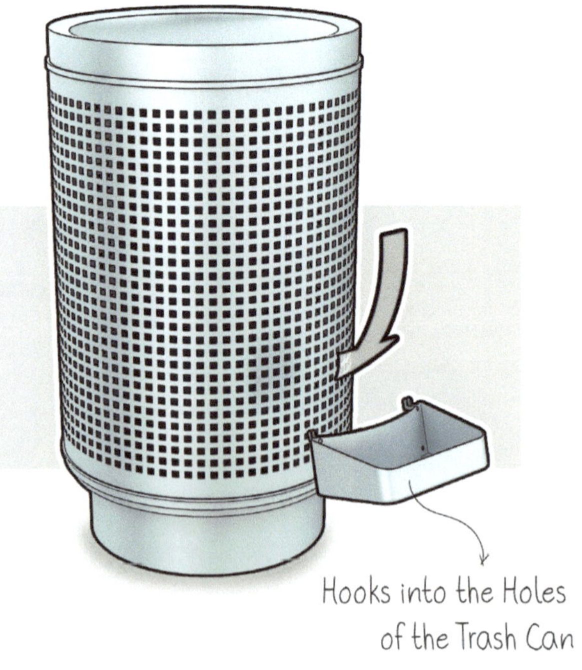

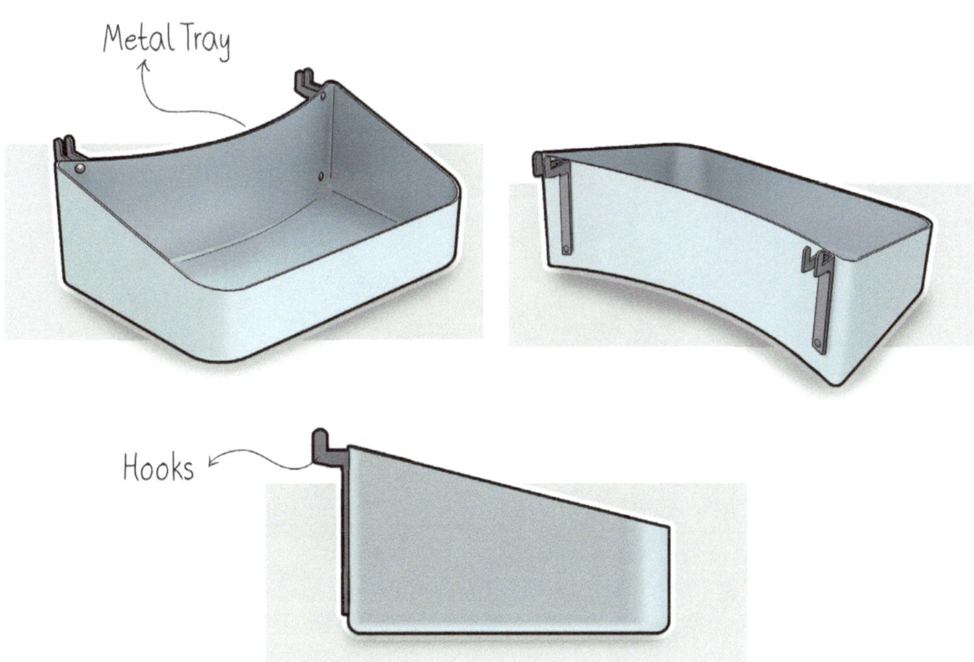
Metal Tray
Hooks

Baggage-Rail System

This concept was inspired by the secure mechanics used in trains while playing with my daughter at a train set, observing how the mechanics effortlessly connect and move multiple railcars. Picture transforming the way you handle your luggage while traveling – a hassle-free and enjoyable experience that resembles assembling a train with carts.

With its smart hitch design at the front and back of each baggage, simply fold down the hitches and with a smooth click, connect all your bags together like a train formation. Now, you have a single unit that you can effortlessly maneuver with just one hand, leaving your other hand free to tend to your child or any other travel essentials.

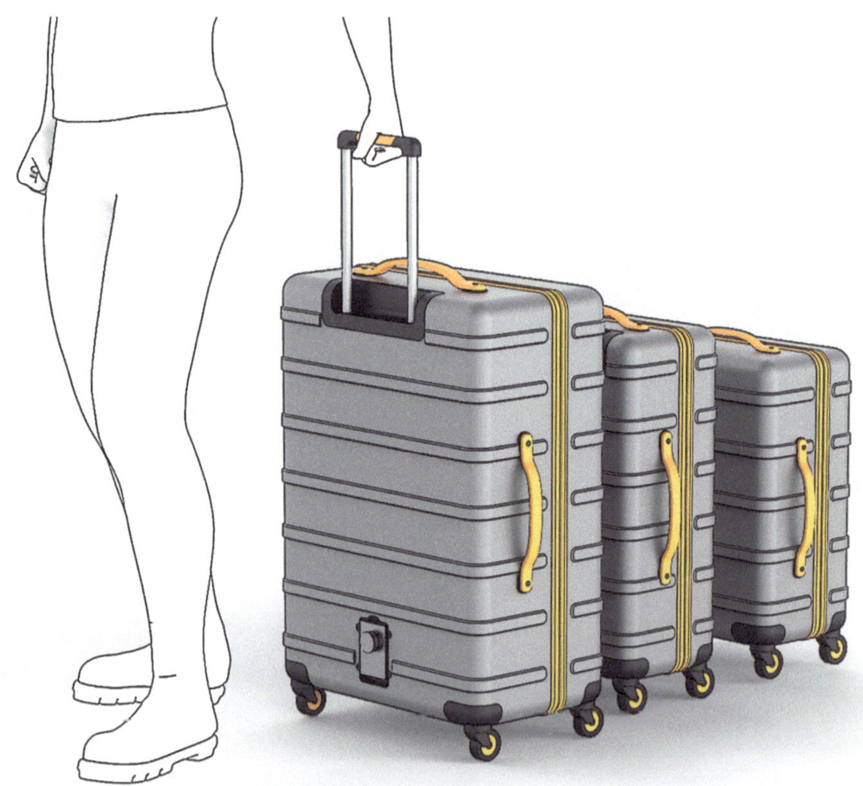

Hitch on the Front

Coupling Mechanism

Adjustable Baby Stroller

Introducing a unique baby stroller concept that offers enhanced convenience. This clever design includes an adjustable handle with a telescopic bar, providing a bit more distance between you and the stroller's rear wheels. Say goodbye to foot discomfort as you enjoy a hassle-free strolling experience with this smart baby stroller. you no longer have to worry about accidentally hitting your feet on the wheels while walking. The innovative design ensures a safer and more comfortable stroll with your little one. Embrace the joy of parenting and explore the world together with this smart baby stroller concept, designed to make your outings more enjoyable and stress-free.

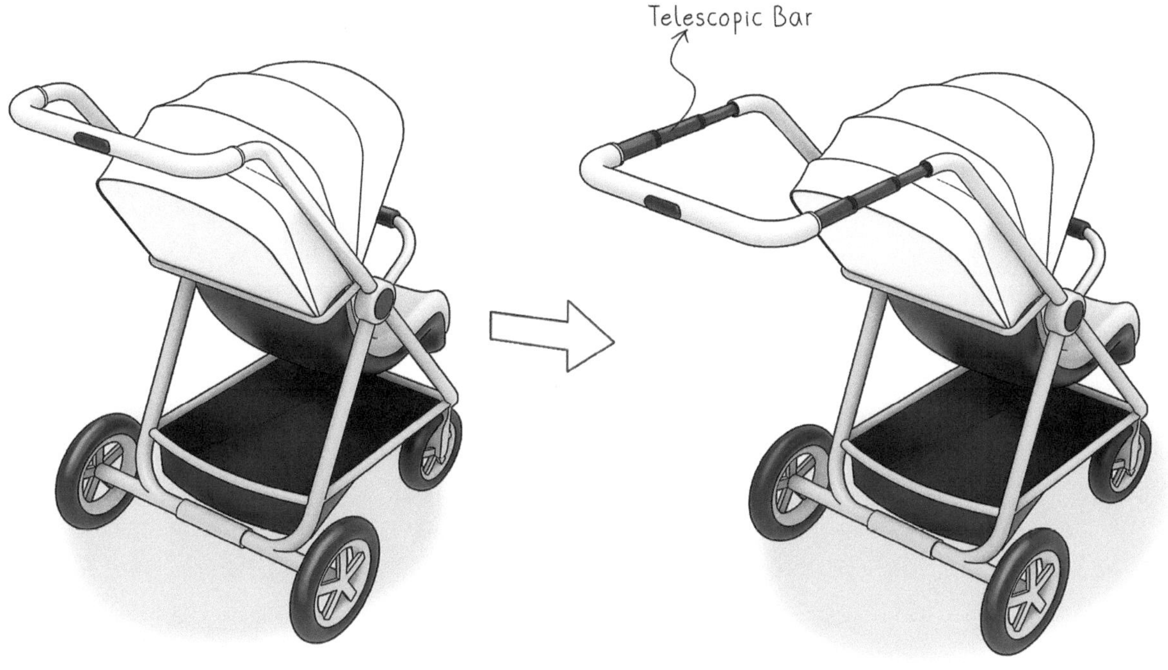
Telescopic Bar

Keeps Feets Away
from Wheels

Electric Grocery Trolley

A thoughtful innovation designed with the elderly in mind, the Electric Grocery Trolley offers a practical solution to ease the burden of carrying heavy loads from the store to their home. It is a grocery trolley equipped with a small electric motor, ready to lend a helping hand. For our beloved elderly shoppers, this trolley becomes an invaluable companion, making their shopping experience smoother and more manageable.

With a gentle push of the handle, the electric motor kicks into action, effortlessly pulling the trolley along. No more struggling to carry heavy bags. The Electric Grocery Trolley empowers the elderly to move freely and independently, ensuring they can comfortably transport their groceries without physical strain.

No Motor Force
When Bag is Empty

Motor Helps Pushing the Load

Bubble Fun Soap

Introducing a playful concept: dish soap that transforms into soap bubbles for kids. The bottle features an attached bubble stick inside the cap, Inspired by the wordplay between "soap bubbles" and "dish soap," this concept captures attention in stores and generates global buzz. Imagine that once you finished using the dish soap, a special gift package contains powder. By mixing it with water in the empty bottle, an instant transformation occurs, converting it into a soap bubble dispenser. This unique experience delivers joy and wonder to children of all ages. This concept not only creates a memorable product but also offers a powerful marketing opportunity. Its distinctiveness and potential for consumer engagement drive interest and excitement.

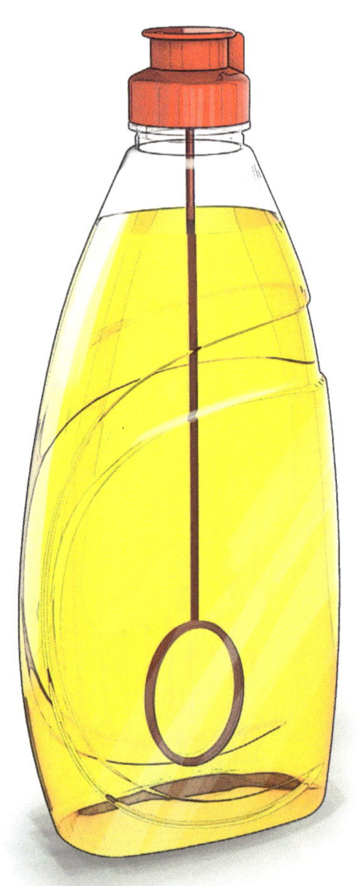

FAIRY

User-Friendly Tool Box

Introducing a practical and user-friendly solution for tool organization. Inspired by a friend's frustrating experience with a power tool box, this concept aims to simplify the process of returning tools to their designated spots. Traditional toolboxes often lack clear indications on how to properly reposition the tools, leading to confusion and disarray.

In this design, using the example of a drill, a visually intuitive solution is implemented. When removing a tool, the silhouette remains visible, serving as a visual guide for its correct reinsertion. By aligning the tool with its corresponding colored outline, users can effortlessly return tools to their designated spots with ease and precision.

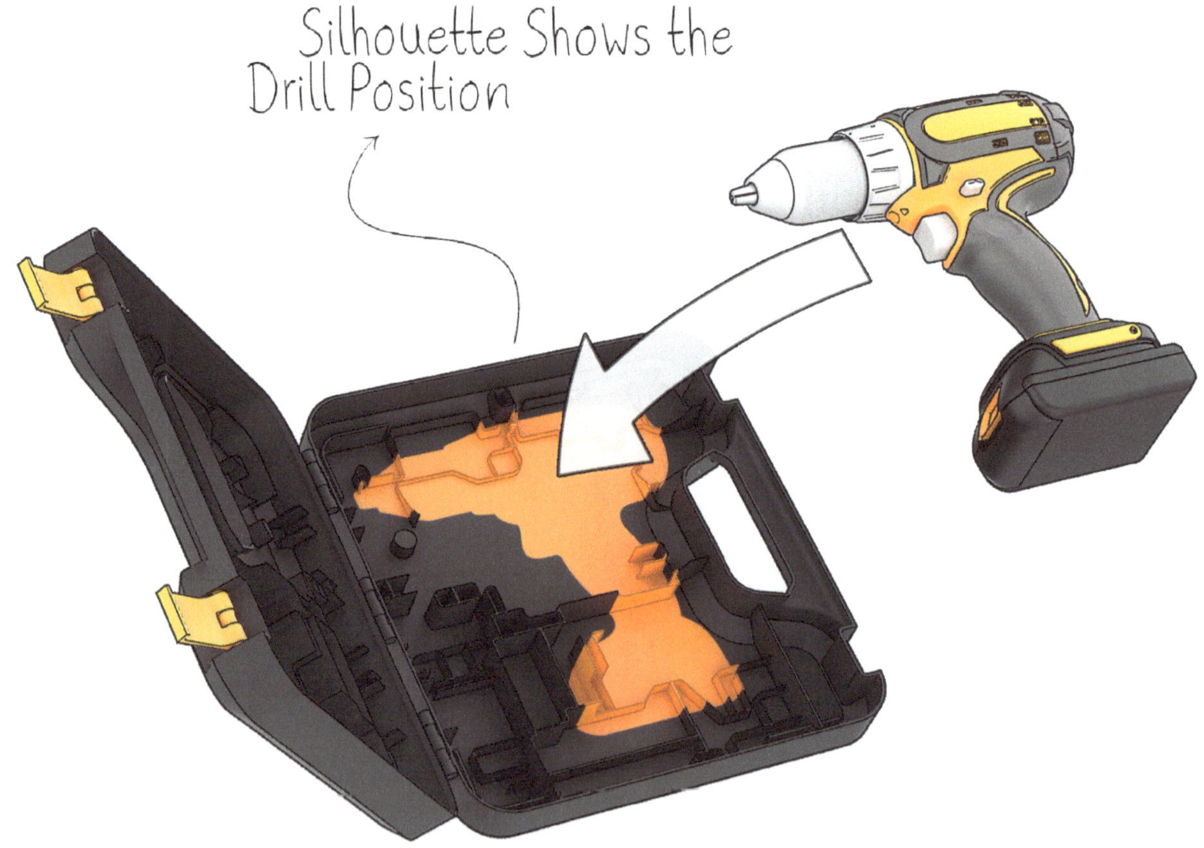

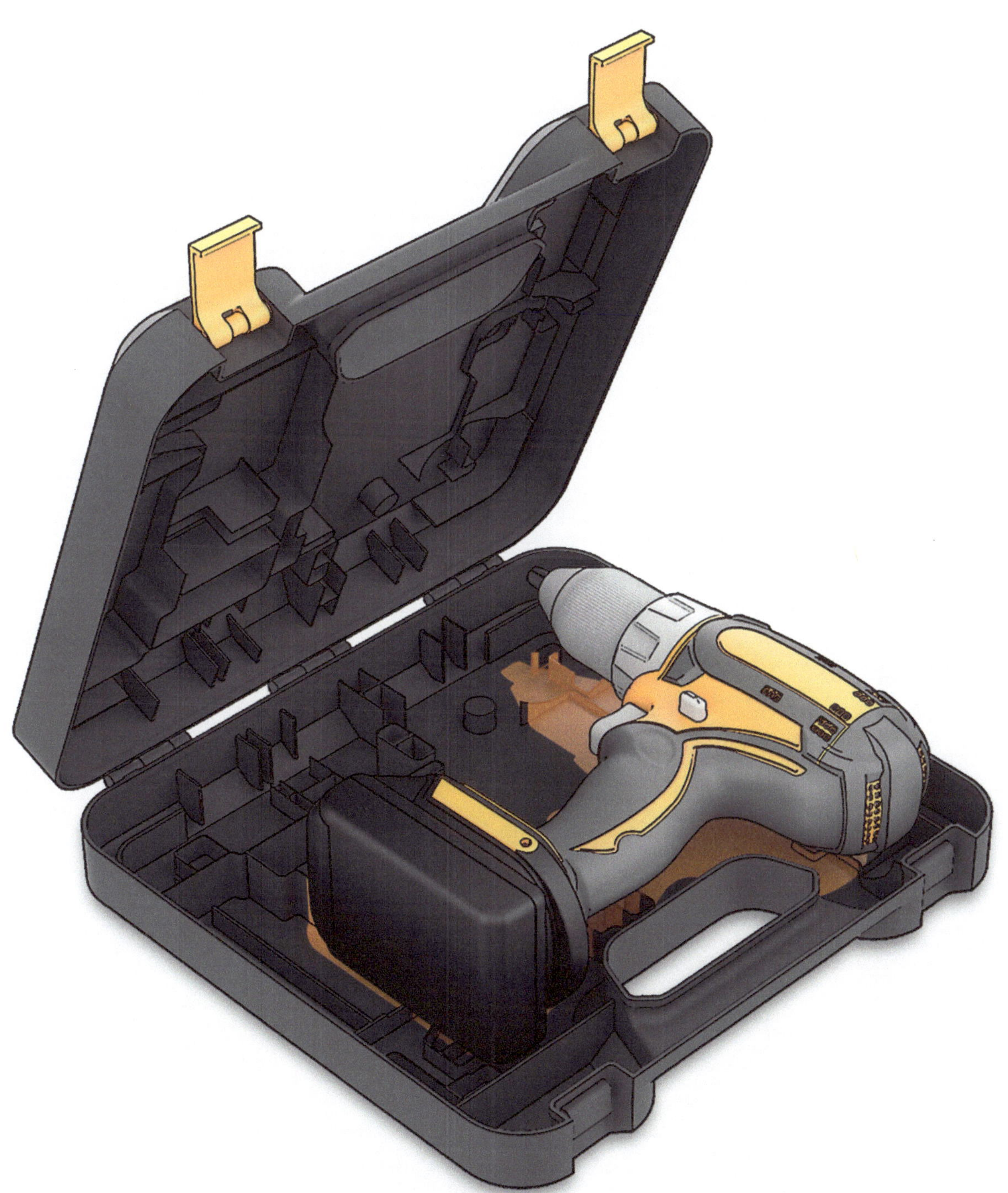

Ice Cream Wrap

Introducing a clever solution for mess-free enjoyment, the ice cream wrap design takes the traditional ice cream eating experience to a new level of convenience. Designed with kids in mind, this innovative concept features a special wrapping that keeps the hands clean while indulging in the delightful treat. By providing a protective layer between the ice cream and little hands, this design ensures a mess-free and enjoyable experience for children. Gone are the days of sticky fingers and messy clean-ups. With the ice cream wrap design, kids can savor their favorite frozen treats with ease and cleanliness, making it a win-win for both kids and parents alike.

Hand Dripping Protection

Tissue Box Compartment

This concept was born out of a personal experience when I found myself sick and constantly in need of tissues. As I battled through a cold and endured frequent sneezing, I noticed a peculiar inconvenience. I would have a tissue box right beside me for quick access, but I ended up using grocery bags as make-shift trash cans to dispose of the used tissues. It felt odd and unsightly. That's when inspiration struck.

I envisioned a tissue box design that incorporate a discreet compartment specifically dedicated to storing and containing the soiled tissues. No longer would we need to resort to makeshift solutions. With this concept, the tissue box becomes a complete and convenient solution for both clean and dirty tissues, ensuring a more seamless and hygienic experience.

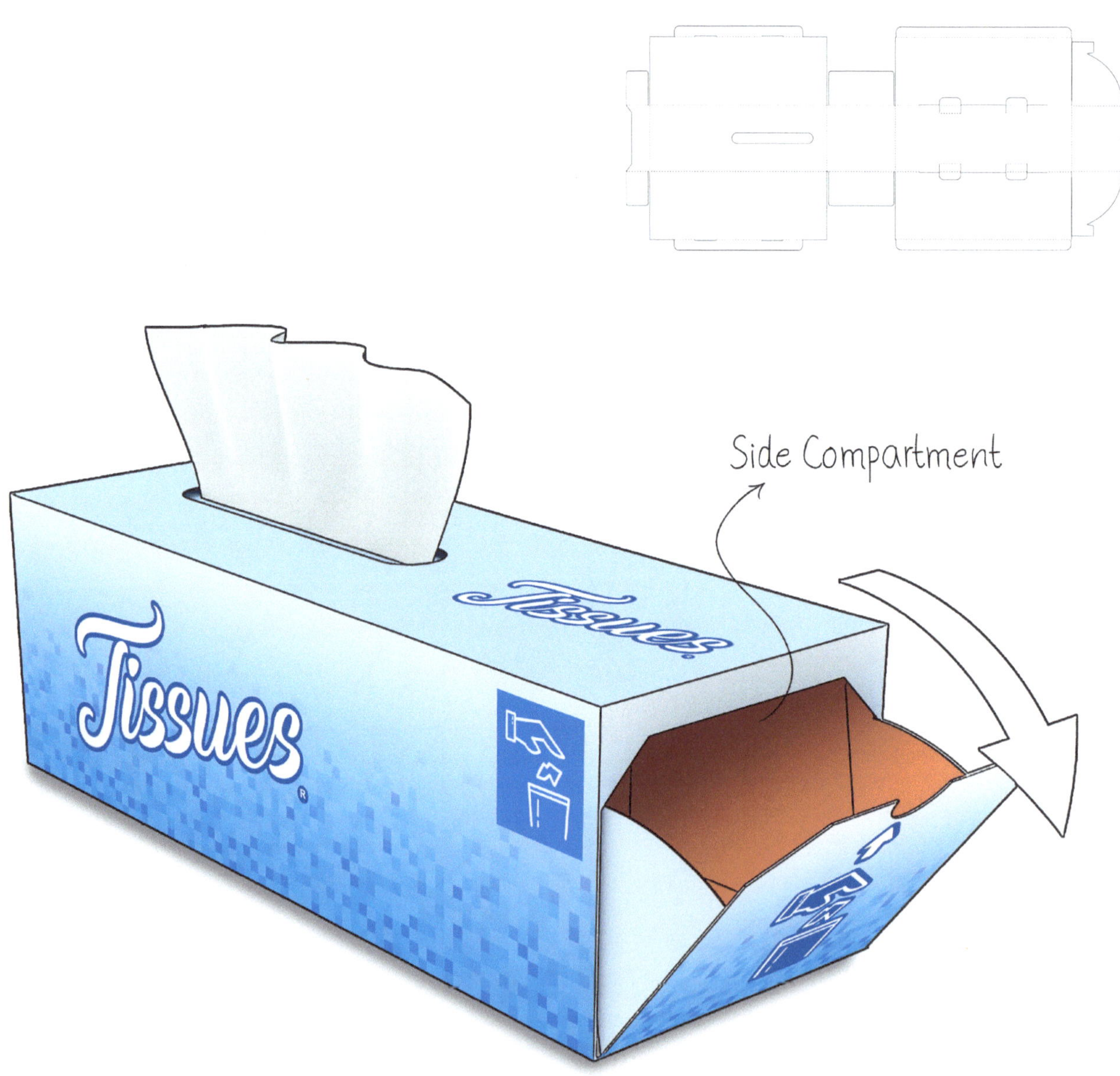

Compartment
for Used Tissues
Tissues
Tissues

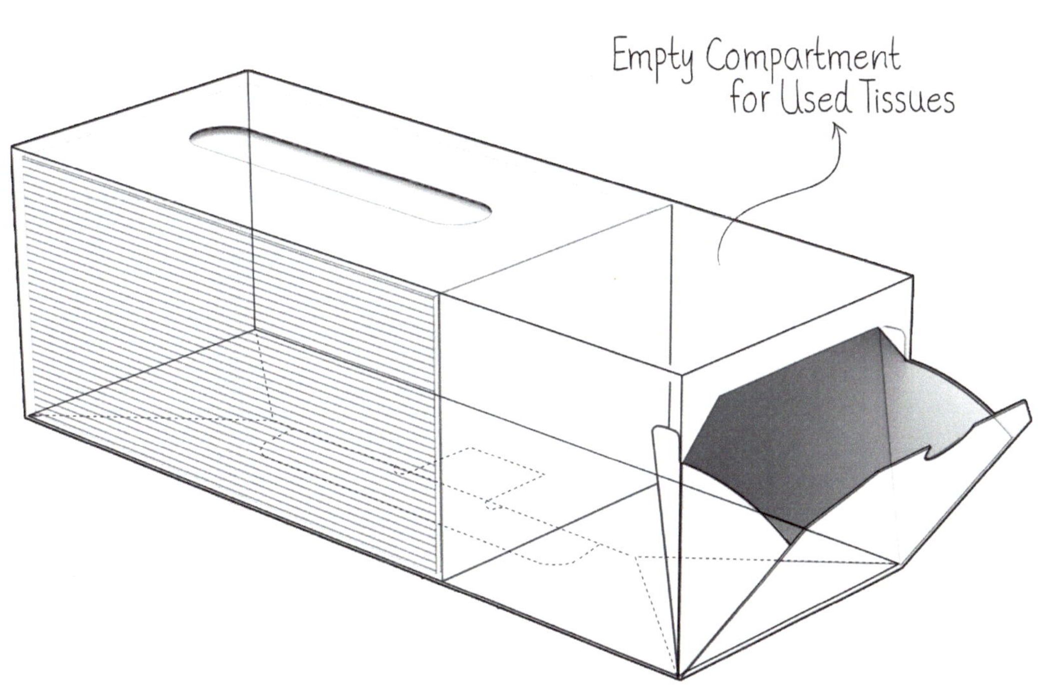
Empty Compartment
for Used Tissues

Sunscreen Mirror

Introducing the "Sunscreen Mirror" – a creative solution to enhance your sun protection experience. Inspired by the observation of common inconveniences at the beach, this innovative concept aims to make applying sunscreen a breeze. The Sunscreen Mirror features a built-in mirror on the lid of the sunscreen container, much like those found in makeup kits. Now, you can easily apply sunscreen to your face without worrying about unwanted residue. Enjoy your time at the beach, confident that your skin is well-protected and free from any cream residue.

Inner Mirror
SUN SCREEN

6-Pack Shoulder Strap

This innovative design features a foldable strap that unfolds into a long, adjustable strap, allowing you to effortlessly carry the weight of the 6-pack on your shoulders, similar to a bag. By redistributing the 8kg load from your wrist and hand to your shoulders and back, this concept provides a practical and ergonomic solution. say goodbye to the discomfort and strain of carrying heavy loads solely with your wrist and hand. With this innovative design, you can enjoy the convenience of evenly distributing the weight, making your journey more comfortable and enjoyable. This concept revolutionizes the way we carry 6-packs, combining functionality with convenience.

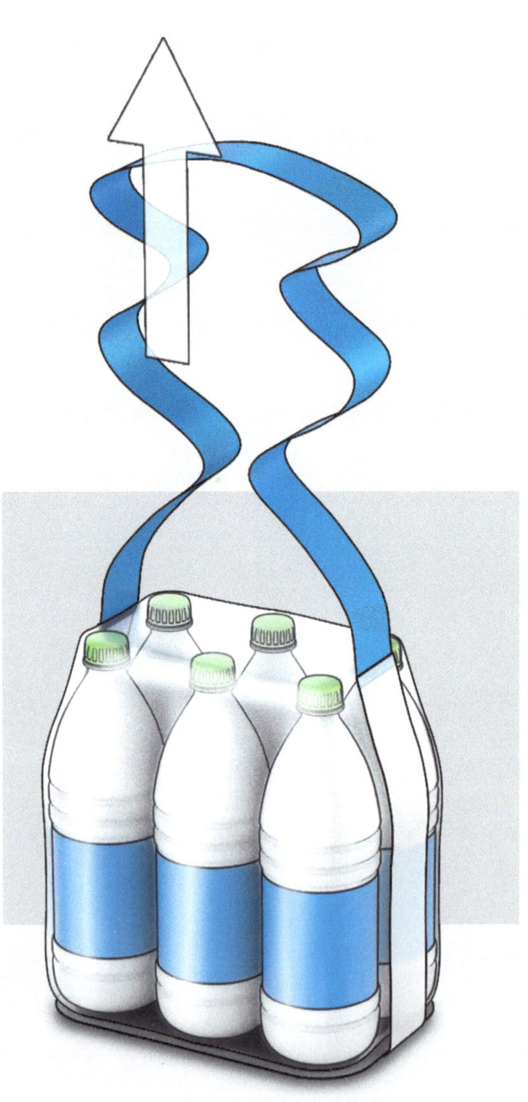

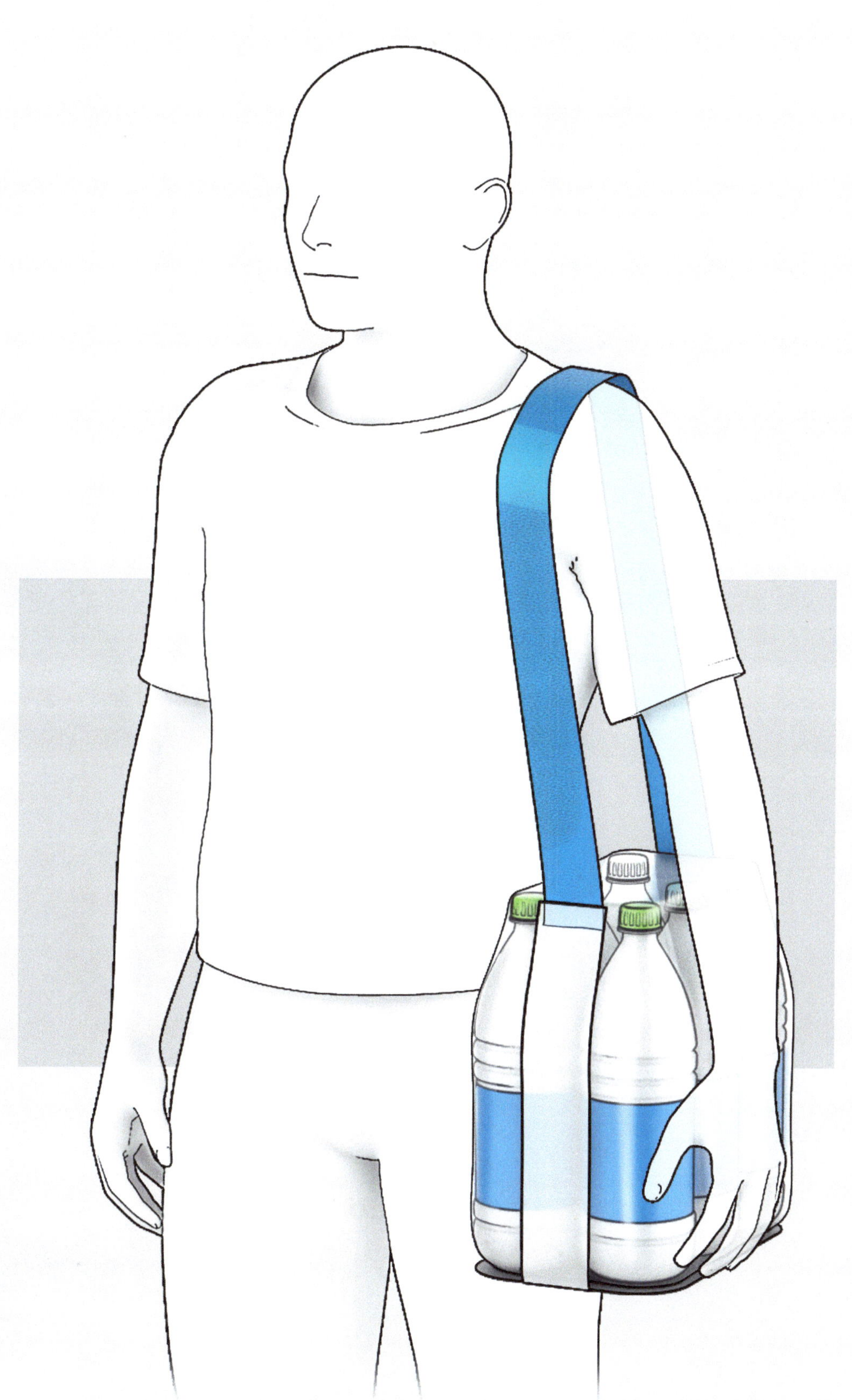

Smart Shoe Tracker

The idea is to add a tracker to a running shoe that displays the number of kilometers it has covered. This concept involves a small LED screen located on the side of the shoe, providing real-time tracking of mileage. The purpose is to address the challenge of keeping track of shoe usage, particularly for runners who use multiple pairs. Many existing tracking apps require manual selection of shoes and

LED Screen

carrying a phone during runs, which can be inconvenient. With this concept, the shoe itself tracks its own kilometers and displays the information on the LED screen. By keeping a close eye on kilometers traveled, runners can accurately assess when it's time to replace their shoes, ensuring optimal performance and reducing the risk of injuries.

Basketball Drill Projector

Introducing an innovative approach to basketball training – the Laser-Projected Play System. Designed to revolutionize the way players learn and execute plays, this system utilizes a laser projector mounted on a stand to display visual diagrams directly on the basketball court. By projecting the plays with recognizable symbols and movements, players, especially kids and young athletes, can easily comprehend and practice complex strategies with precision. The Laser-Projected Play System offers numerous benefits to players and coaches alike. With real-time visualization of plays during practice, players can

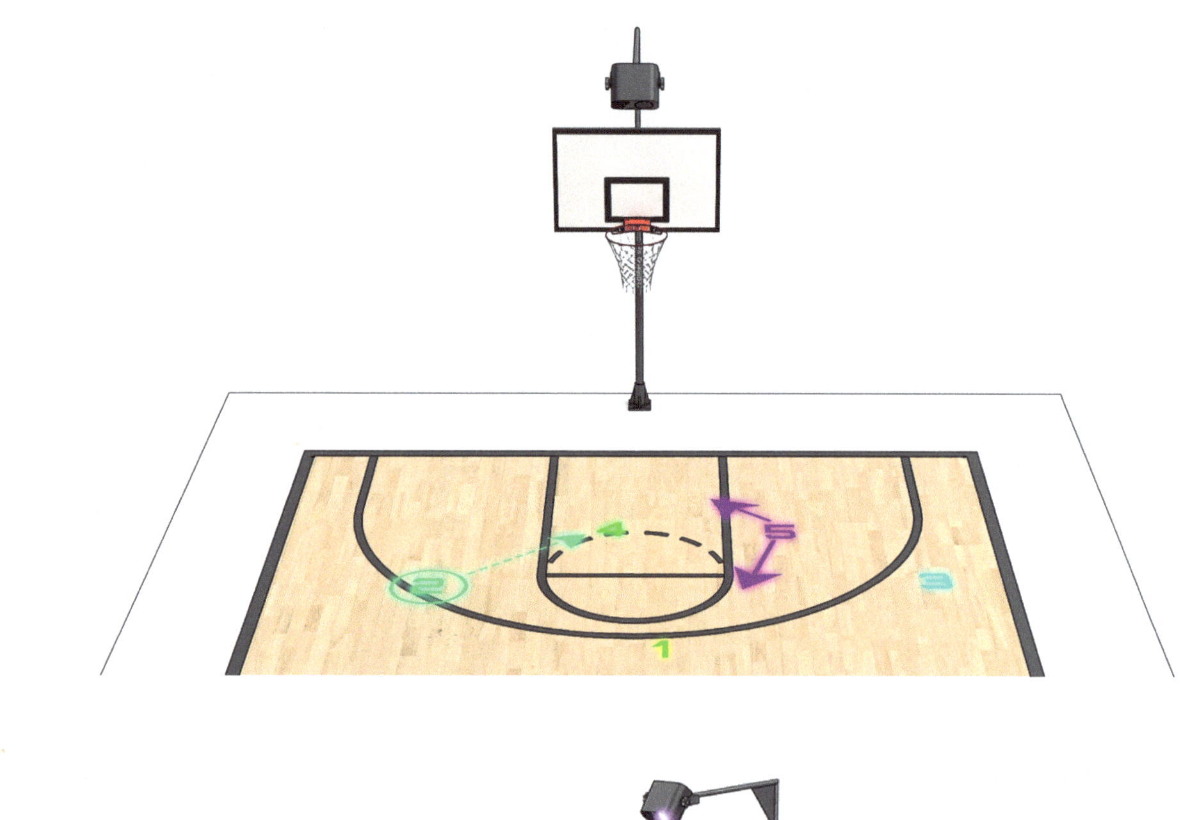

develop better spatial awareness, positioning, and decision-making skills. The interactive nature of the system engages players and enhances their learning experience, making training sessions more enjoyable and effective. Coaches can conveniently select from a wide range of plays through an iPad or app, tailoring the training to suit their team's needs and skill levels. This cutting-edge solution elevates the quality of basketball training, empowering players to master plays, boost confidence, and excel on the court.

Snake Extension Wire

The snake-inspired extension cord offers a fun and creative twist on the ordinary. Breaking away from the plain white cables typically found in stores, this concept brings a touch of excitement and uniqueness to the forefront. The idea originated when I needed an extension cord, and the realization dawned that they all looked remarkably similar. Inspired by the inherent resemblance to a snake, the concept began to take shape. Drawing cues from the captivating patterns found on snake skins, the vision emerged:

an extension cord designed to embody the essence of a snake. Taking inspiration from the vibrant colors and distinct patterns of the corn snake, commonly found throughout the southeastern and central United States, this concept found its muse in the natural world. This playful twist transforms the mundane into an eye-catching statement piece. While it may not appeal to those with a fear of snakes, for those who embrace the charm and whimsy, this snake-inspired extension cord becomes a delightful addition to their

spaces. It serves as an example of how even the most overlooked and taken-for-granted products can be transformed into objects of fun and creativity. As you explore the boundaries of design, consider the potential for creativity and innovation in even the simplest of products. This concept not only inspires you to think outside the box but also encourages you to embark on a journey of observation and discovery. Challenge yourself to visit stores, examine the products, and identify those that appear strikingly similar across brands. Then, let your creativity soar as you find ways to make them unique, just like the snake-inspired extension cord.

Pool Cue Chalk

Introducing a unique twist on pool cue chalk – snooker chalk in cool and humorous designs. Departing from the conventional rectangular box shape, this concept brings a touch of playfulness to the world of chalk. Imagine pool cue chalk molded into the shape of a skull, nose, or other amusing designs.

Gone are the days of mundane blue squares that blend into the background. With these funny and eye-catching designs, your pool table becomes a canvas for self-expression and adds an element of fun to your games.

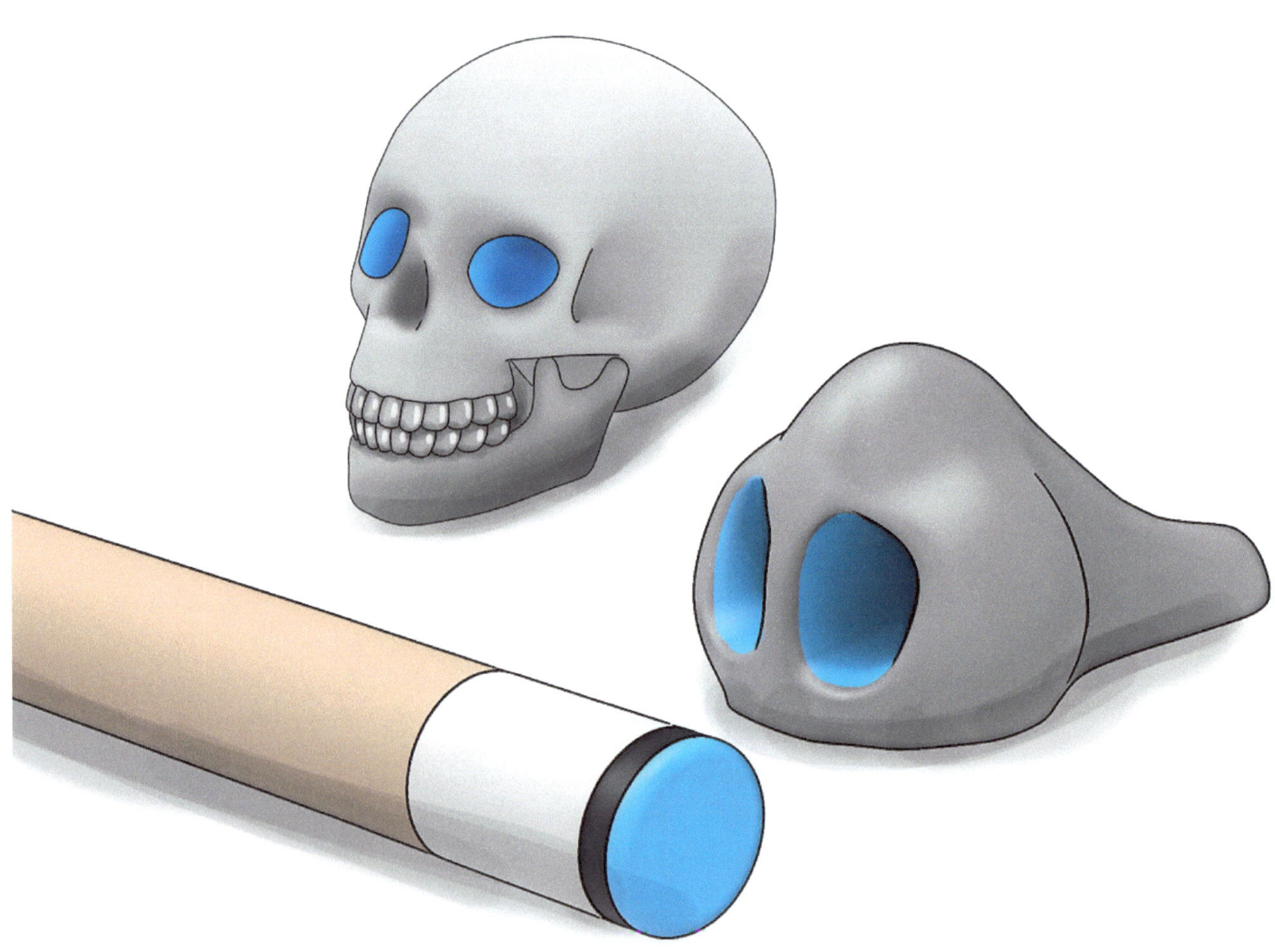

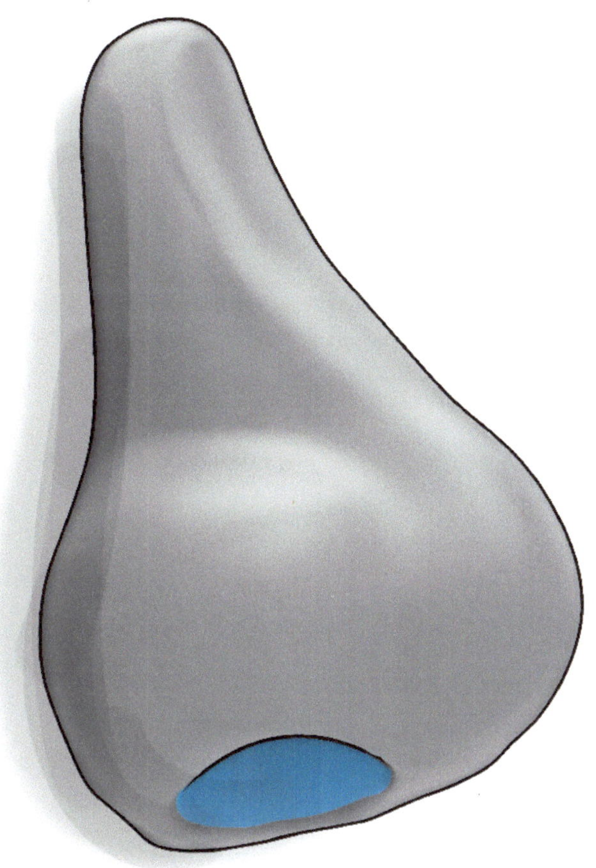

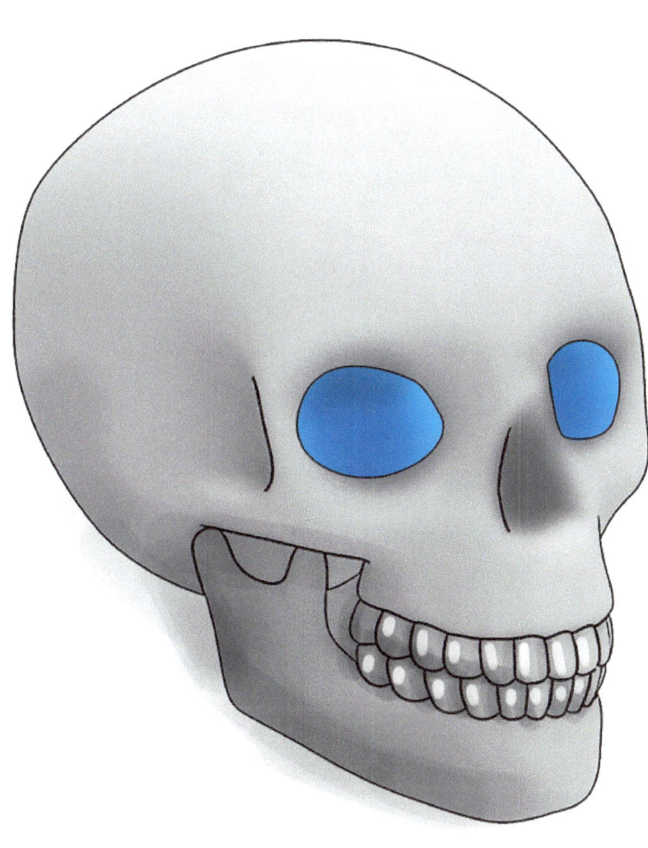

Gym Dumbbell Door

Introducing a unique twist on pool cue chalk – snooker chalk in cool and humorous designs. Departing from the conventional rectangular box shape, this concept brings a touch of playfulness to the world of chalk. Imagine pool cue chalk molded into the shape of a skull, nose, or other amusing designs.

Gone are the days of mundane blue squares that blend into the background. With these funny and eye-catching designs, your pool table becomes a canvas for self-expression and adds an element of fun to your games.

Gym Door